A Photographic Guide to the
Shieldbugs and Squashbugs
of the British Isles

Martin Evans and Roger Edmondson

Published by WGUK

To Mark

This is the sea

Mark.

First Published 2005 by WGUK in association with WildGuideUK.com

© Text: Martin Evans and Roger Edmondson

© Photographs: Martin Evans

ISBN 0-9549506-0-7

Printed and bound by The Charlesworth Group, Wakefield, UK

Photographs: Front cover: *Eurydema dominulus*
              Title page: *Eysarcoris aeneus*
              Back cover: *Palomena prasina*

Contents

Acknowledgements

We would like to thank a number of people for assisting us with this book.

Janet and Jim Boyd for the use of specimens, their hospitality and encouragement.

Ray Barnett, the Collections Manager of the Bristol City Museum and Art Gallery, for the use of specimens from his private collection, as well as that of the Museum. We also thank him for proof reading and making many helpful suggestions.

Dr.Mike Wilson, the Head of Entomology at the National Museum and Galleries of Wales in Cardiff, for allowing us to use the facilities and collections, and for his enthusiasm and encouragement. Also we thank Mark Pavett and the other staff and volunteers in Cardiff for their friendly encouragement and discussions.

Richard Southwood, Dennis Leston and Frederick Warne and Co. Ltd for the inspirational 'Land and Water Bugs of the British Isles', and also Roger Hawkins for a more recent publication, the excellent 'Shieldbugs of Surrey'.

Finally we thank: Carolyn and Amy,

Kate, Tessa, Nancy and George

for putting up with us and for their understanding of our fascination with creatures such as shieldbugs…. Well, we think they understand?

Foreword

For a number of years Martin Evans and myself, have been carrying out environmental surveys for the Bristol Regional Environmental Records Centre (BRERC). These have been predominantly plant based, but we have also recorded the birds, butterflies, moths, mammals and insects that we have come across.

Martin has been taking photographs since the early 1980s, of moths in particular, but also of any plants or insects that took his fancy. When we finished surveying last summer, we were trying to decide what to do next. The obvious choice was to make use of his photographs for publication. Various groups of insects were considered and several projects are in hand.

However, the shieldbugs stood out. Here was a group of insects that were identifiable without having to dissect them. Many of them are fairly common in the southern half of the British Isles and yet there is a distinct lack of readily available literature and photographs to identify them. This was something that we could set our minds to.

We checked through our existing photographs, including those on the website at WildGuideUK.com, to see how many species we already had. There were quite a few and we thought we might be able to produce an incomplete, but still useful, printed photographic guide. Our next aim was to find and photograph as many more species as we could before the end of the season.

We never thought that we would be able to photograph all of the British species, but with the help of friends, we aimed to get as many as possible. Janet and Jim Boyd and Ray Barnett made their collections available to us and Ray mentioned in passing that we ought to contact Mike Wilson at the National Museum of Wales.

This was a breakthrough for us, as we now had available a large number of specimens to study and photograph. After searching the collection, we found that we had every native species except for one. We told Mike that we only had *Bathysolen nubilus* missing. Unprompted, he made a phone call to Sheila Brooke, who to our amazement was able to supply one to the museum within a couple of weeks. Thank you for that Sheila. We now had photographs of all the native species.

Our aim with this book was not to produce an in-depth view of the current status of British shieldbugs, but more to produce a book that will enable us to simply and easily identify the shieldbugs that we come across. In doing so we hope we have made it easier for others to do the same.

Roger Edmondson 2005

Introduction

Plants, birds and mammals have a large following with those interested in natural history, but very few insects appear to inspire any lasting interest. Only butterflies, dragonflies and more recently moths attract the long term attention of anyone other than conservationists and entomologists.

If you asked a member of the public to name some British insects, he or she might include Peacock butterfly, Red Admiral or 'Cabbage' White and perhaps, if they were knowledgeable, a dragonfly or a hawk-moth. It is unlikely that they would name any of the shieldbugs or squashbugs.

This is a shame as they form a reasonably small and manageable group to study. It is easy to get started, as many are present even in suburban gardens and are common in the wider countryside. There are also a number that are exotic in shape or colour and have interesting lifecycles, so they can be very rewarding. As well as those, there are also scarce species for the more dedicated naturalist, who will be guided to many interesting habitats and find a great challenge in looking for them.

In researching this book it was surprising how difficult it was to find pictures of the less common species. Hours spent searching the worldwide web would bring up species lists from all over the northern hemisphere, but rarely a good photograph. If a picture was found then it was usually part of a gallery of natural history photographs without any associated text.

This book should help with this deficit of information and hopefully increase the interest in these insects. All of the thirty-three resident shieldbugs and ten squashbugs are illustrated, each with a full page plate. Opposite the plate there is a brief account of their identifying features and life history.

Accurate identification is a problem for many people, as they are put off by text keys, so a picture key has been used in this guide, which will either take the reader directly to the correct species account, or that of a very similar species from where the correct species can be identified.

For convenience there is a life history table near the end of the book. This can be used as a quick guide to which species are likely to be found if the reader is visiting a specific habitat at a particular time of year.

The production of this book has brought up many questions, some of which even a novice may be able to answer with a small amount of study. For instance is the variation of colour and pattern in the genera *Odontoscelis* and *Rhacognathus* related to their sex? Are the life cycles of these bugs being affected by global warming? What is the distribution of these species in your area? These are questions that would be interesting to research and could also make a valuable contribution to shieldbug conservation.

Hemiptera; the true bugs

Although the word 'bug' is commonly used for almost any insect, the Hemiptera are the true bugs.

The order **Hemiptera** consists of three main suborders; Heteroptera, Sternorrhyncha and Auchenorrhyncha, with around 80,000 species worldwide and over 1,700 having been recorded in Britain. They are variable in form, but nearly all have piercing mouthparts, known as the rostrum, for sucking the juices from either plants or animals (depending on the species of bug). The adults usually have two pairs of wings, with the forewings in many cases hardened, although some species have reduced wings or no wings at all.

The **Heteroptera** number over 500 species in Britain. They have hardened bases to the forewings with membranous tips, while the hindwings are membranous throughout. The wings are folded flat over the abdomen and the antennae have up to five segments. The rostrum appears to arise from the front of the head, as there is cuticle behind it known as the gula.

Amongst others, this suborder contains the Pentatomidae (shieldbugs), Tingidae (lace bugs), Miridae (capsid bugs), Nabidae (damsel bugs), Anthocoridae (flower bugs), Lygaeidae (ground bugs) and the aquatic bugs such as the Notonectidae (water boatmen).

The **Sternorrhyncha** and **Auchenorrhyncha** may have hardened or membranous forewings, but they are usually uniform throughout. The hind wings are membranous. The wings are folded over the abdomen in a tent-like manner and the antennae are variable in the number of segments. The Sternorrhyncha and Auchenorrhyncha do not have a gula so the rostrum is set back underneath the head.

The **Sternorrhyncha** have the rostrum set far back (appearing to originate between the front legs) and have no more than two segments to the tarsi (feet) in adults. The Sternorrhyncha contains the Aleyrodidae (whiteflies), Aphidoidea (aphids), Coccoidea (scale insects and mealybugs etc) and similar species.

The **Auchenorrhyncha** have the rostrum below the head and have three segments to the tarsi of the adults. This suborder includes the Delphacidae (planthoppers), Cercopidae (froghoppers or spittlebugs), Cicadidae (cicadas), Cicadellidae (leafhoppers) and Membracidae (treehoppers).

The Hemiptera have a large economic effect on man. The planthoppers, aphids, scale insects and others are major pests of horticulture, agriculture and forestry and are the main vectors of plant pathogenic viruses. Some species are even human parasites (such as the blood sucking Common Bed Bug *Cimex lectularius*).

This is not the whole picture, as the Hemiptera are not all bad. Most bugs, because of their choice of food plants are not pests. Many of the predacious species have a positive effect on man, as they eat the larva and adults of invertebrates that are themselves agricultural pests.

The British Shieldbugs and Squashbugs

The thirty-two native (plus one newly naturalised) British shieldbugs belong to five different families within the super-family Pentatomoidea:

Acanthosomatidae -four species in the genera *Acanthosoma*, *Cyphostethus, Elasmostethus* and *Elasmucha.*

Scutelleridae -four species in the genera *Odontoscelis* and *Eurygaster.*

Cynidae -seven species in the genera *Legnotus, Geotomus, Tritomegas* and *Sehirus*

Thyreocoridae - with just one species in the genus *Thyreocoris.*

Pentatomidae -seventeen species in the genera *Podops, Sciocoris, Aelia, Neottiglossa, Eysarcoris, Palomena, Nezara, Dolycoris, Piezodorus, Pentatoma, Eurydema, Picromerus, Troilus, Rhacognathus* and *Zicrona.*

There are also at least a dozen other species of shieldbug that have been migrants, vagrants or have been at least temporarily established in Britain.

These insects are called shieldbugs because of their shield-like shape when adult. They have a large scutellum usually reaching the membranous area of the wing-tip. They are all macropterous (fully winged) and have three segments to the tarsi (feet) and five segments in their antennae. They are sometimes known as stink bugs, because of the strong odour that is emitted by some species when they are threatened. Although most of them are vegetarian, some such as *Troilus luridus* are predators.

Most shieldbugs over-winter as adults and may become a darker colour at that time of year. The familiar Green Shieldbug *Palomena prasina* is an example of this, as it is actually brown during the winter. It quickly regains the green colouration when it becomes active in the spring.

The Gorse Shieldbug *Piezodorus lituratus* also changes its colour during the winter. As an immature adult in the late summer, it has red and purple markings. When it has fully matured and is reproductively viable in the spring, these colours have been replaced by an overall yellowish-green.

The larvae of the shieldbugs may look entirely different than the adults and even vary from one instar (phase between larval skin changes) to another. Many of these larvae (or nymphs) are illustrated in the shieldbug species accounts in this guide, as are some of the different instars.

Many shieldbugs have an interesting life history. The Parent Bug *Elasmucha grisea* is so named because the female broods her eggs and young, guarding them against predators and parasites. Perhaps less well known is that many other species of shieldbug also exhibit brood care, including the Pied Shieldbug *Tritomegas bicolor.*

Another perhaps surprising fact, is that many of these bugs stridulate, using a special process on each wing called a strigil. *Sciocoris cursitans* is an example of this. It reportedly stridulates quite loudly for its size.

There are ten British squashbugs. They belong to the family Coreidae and are superficially similar to the shieldbugs, although they are generally yellow-brown to grey in colour and narrower in form, with a laterally expanded abdomen. They feed mainly on fruit and seeds and get their common name from the United States of America where some species are a pest of squash fruits.

The habitat of several of the squashbugs is sparse vegetation and bare ground. The importance of this habitat is often not appreciated even by conservationists. There are many other species of bug as well as a large number of bees, ants, beetles and grasshoppers that live in areas of eroded grassland or bare ground. The long term future of these and a great number of other invertebrates is dependent on the conservation of this habitat.

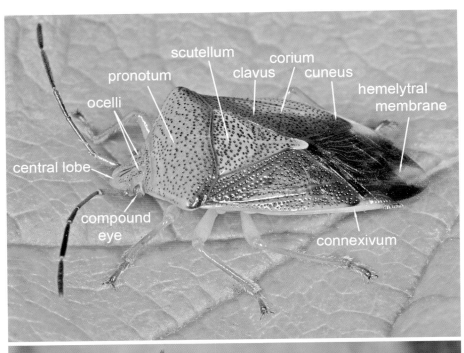
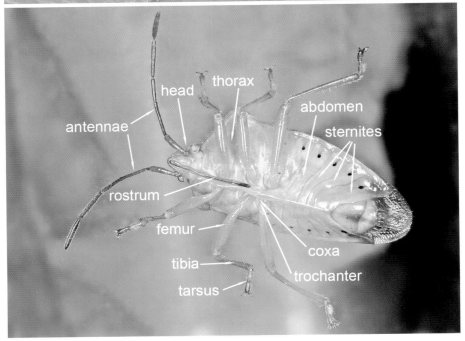

Anatomy of a Shieldbug

Abdomen: the rear section of the body.

Antenna(e): these are segmented and vary in the number of segments according to the family (five in Pentatomidae).

Central lobe: the head is divided into three lobes. The shape and size of the central lobe is a useful identification feature in several species.

Clavus: the inner part of the wing adjacent to the scutellum.

Compound eye: multi-faceted (has many lenses). The eyes are positioned on each side of the head.

Connexivum: lateral extension of the abdomen.

Corium: the main area of the toughened and opaque base of the forewing.

Coxa: the first small segment (from the body) of the leg.

Cuneus: the most distal part of the toughened and opaque base of the forewing.

Distal: furthest from the base.

Dorsal or **Dorsum**: the upper surface of the insect.

Femur (plural –**femora**): the third division (large upper section) of the leg.

Hemelytron: this is the forewing of heteropteron bugs (including the shieldbugs).

These bugs have their wings divided into two parts:

-the toughened basal part which consists of the **corium, clavus** and **cuneus.** There are 'fractures' between these areas which give flexibility to the wing.

-the distal part which consists of the **hemyletral membrane** (the clear tip).

Instar: the larval stage between two successive skin moults. There are several instars and the larva may have an entirely different pattern or colour during each instar.

Legs: consisting of fore-legs, mid-legs and hind-legs. Each of these is divided into 5 parts: (from the base) the **coxa, trochanter, femur, tibia** and **tarsus**.

Ocelli: these two organs on the top of the head are simple eyes (some Hemiptera have three).

Ovum (plural **ova**): the egg.

Oviposite: to lay eggs.

Pronotum: this is the large structure saddling the thorax. In many of the shield bugs it is has thorn-like lateral extensions.

Punctures: small depressions over the surface of the bug.

Rostrum: the modified mouthparts, which are used for piercing and sucking plant or animal matter. In the Heteroptera the rostrum is at the front of the head (as in the glossary picture of the Birch Shieldbug). This is due to a projection of the cuticle behind it called the **gula**. The Sternorrhyncha and Auchenorrhyncha do not have a gula, so their rostrums are set back under the head. How far it is set back defines to which suborder the bug belongs.

Scutellum: this is the central plate set at the back of the pronotum. The scutellum is usually triangular, but is sometimes parallel sided and enlarged. It totally covers the wings in some species.

Sternites: plates on the ventral surface of the abdomen.

Stridulation: rubbing two parts of the body together to produce a noise or 'song'.

Strigil: a structure on the wing of some bugs that is used for stridulation.

Tarsus (plural –**tarsi**): the foot, fifth or last division of the leg (which is itself segmented). There are three segments to the tarsus in the Pentatomidae.

Tergites: plates on the dorsal surface of the abdomen.

Thorax: the middle section of the body behind the head and in front of the abdomen.

Tibia (plural –**tibiae**): the fourth division (from the body) of the leg. The section between the femur and the tarsus.

Trochanter: the second small segment (from the body) of the leg.

Tubercles: small raised 'bumps' scattered over the surface of the insect. They may have hairs protruding from them.

Ventral: the underside of the insect.

Picture Keys

The following pictures include all of the British shieldbugs (Pentatomidae), some of the commoner shieldbug larvae and finally all of the British squashbugs (Coreidae). It is intended as a quick reference to aid identification.

Acanthosoma haemorrhoidale
Hawthorn Shieldbug
Page 22   13 to 15mm

Cyphostethus tristriatus
Juniper Shieldbug
Page 24   9.5 to 10mm

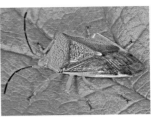

Elasmostethus interstinctus
Birch Shieldbug
Page 26   8 to 11.5mm

Elasmucha grisea
Parent Bug
Page 28   7 to 9mm

Odontoscelis fuliginosa
Page 30   6 to 8mm

Odontoscelis lineola
Page 32   4 to 6mm

Eurygaster maura

Page 34   8.5 to 10mm

Eurygaster testudinaria

Page 36   9 to 11mm

Legnotus limbosus

Page 38   3.5 to 4.5mm

Legnotus picipes

Page 40   3 to 4mm

Geotomus punctulatus

Page 42   3.5mm to 4.5mm

Tritomegas bicolor
Pied Shieldbug
Page 44   5.5 to 7.5mm

Canthophorus impressus

Page 46   6 to 7mm

Sehirus biguttatus

Page 48   5 to 6.5mm

Sehirus luctuosus

Page 50   7 to 9mm

Thyreocoris scarabaeoides
Negro Bug
Page 52   3 to 4mm

Podops inuncta

Page 54   5.5 to 6mm

Sciocoris cursitans

Page 56   4.5 to 6mm

Aelia acuminata
Bishop's Mitre
Page 58   8 to 9mm

Neottiglossa pusilla

Page 60   4 to 4.5mm

Eysarcoris fabricii

Page 62   5 to 7mm

Eysarcoris aeneus

Page 64   5 to 6mm

Palomena prasina
Green Shieldbug (winter)
Page 66   12 to 13.5mm

Palomena prasina
Green Shieldbug (summer)
Page 66   12 to 13.5mm

Nezara viridula
Southern Green Shieldbug
Page 68   11 to 15mm

Dolycoris baccarum
Sloe Bug
Page 70   11 to 12mm

Piezodorus lituratus
Gorse Shieldbug (late summer)
Page 72   10 to 13mm

Piezodorus lituratus
Gorse Shieldbug (spring)
Page 72   10 to 13mm

Pentatoma rufipes
Forest Bug
Page 74   11 to 14mm

Eurydema oleracea
Brassica Bug (pale form)
Page 76   6 to 7mm

Eurydema oleracea
Brassica Bug (red form)
Page 76   6 to 7mm

Eurydema dominulus

Page 78   6 to 7mm

Picromerus bidens

Page 80   12 to 13.5mm

Troilus luridus

Page 82   10 to 12mm

Rhacognathus punctatus
Heather Bug
Page 84   7 to 9mm

Zicrona caerulea
Blue Bug
Page 86   5 to 7mm

Acanthosoma haemorrhoidale
Hawthorn Shieldbug   larva
Page 22

Elasmostethus interstinctus
Birch Shieldbug   larva
Page 26

Eurygaster testudinaria
                    larva
Page 36

Tritomegas bicolor
Pied Shieldbug   larva
Page 44

Aelia acuminata
Bishop's Mitre   larva
Page 58

Eysarcoris fabricii
                    larva
Page 62

Palomena prasina
Green Shieldbug   larva
Page 66

Dolycoris baccarum
Sloe Bug   larva
Page 70

Piezodorus lituratus
Gorse Shieldbug   larva
Page 72

Pentatoma rufipes
Forest Bug   larva
Page 74

Troilus luridus
                    larva
Page 82

Zicrona caerulea
Blue Bug   larva
Page 86

Gonocerus acuteangulatus
Box Bug
Page 88   11 to 14mm

Coreus marginatus

Page 90   13 to 15mm

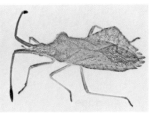

Syromastes rhombeus

Page 92   9.5 to 10.5mm

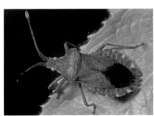

Enoplops scapha

Page 94   11 to 12mm

Spathocera dahlmanni

Page 96   5 to 6.5mm

Bathysolen nubilus

Page 98   5.5 to 7mm

Arenocoris falleni

Page 100   6 to 7mm

Arenocoris waltli

Page 102   7 to 7.5mm

Ceraleptus lividus

Page 104   9 to 11mm

Coriomeris denticulatus

Page 106   7 to 9mm

Coreus marginatus
                                                larva
Page 90

Species Accounts

Acanthosomatidae

Acanthosoma haemorrhoidale (Linnaeus, 1758)

Hawthorn Shieldbug

ID features: A large brightly coloured bug, with red lateral extensions to the pronotum and a red tip to the abdomen.

Adult: August until early July.

Length: 13 to 15mm.

Larvae: Late May until late September feeding on the leaves and fruit of Hawthorn *Crataegus monogyna*, oak *Quercus* spp., birch *Betula* spp., poplar *Populus* spp., Hazel *Corylus avellana* and many other trees.

Habitat: A woodland species, although it may be found in gardens and parks if they are populated with trees.

Distribution: Common throughout most of Britain and Ireland, but scarce in Scotland.

Similar species

Elasmostethus interstinctus (page 26) is smaller with less colourful and less pointed lateral extensions to the pronotum.

Cyphostethus tristriatus (page 24) is much smaller without the red points on the pronotum. It has pink-brown boomerang-shaped markings on the forewings.

Pictures 1.to 3.adults, 4.late instar larvae, 5.last instar larva

Acanthosomatidae

Cyphostethus tristriatus (Fabricius, 1787)

Juniper Shieldbug

ID features: A yellow-green bug with a distinctive pink-brown boomerang-shaped marking on the corium.

Adult: Late August until June.

Length: 9.5 to 10mm.

Larvae: The larvae feed on ripe, second year, Juniper berries *Juniperus communis*, and are also known to occur on Lawson Cypress *Chamaecyparis lawsoniana*. They are more oval in shape than the adult. The head is green with black speckling and marked with two vertical black lines. The pronotum is also green with black speckling. The abdomen is bright green with a large yellow, black and tan marking in the centre and small black marks around the connexivum.

Habitat: Originally a species of southern Juniper woodlands, but with the availability of Juniper in garden centres this bug is now becoming a common garden species in the south of England.

Distribution: Southern and midland counties of England and possibly expanding its range.

Similar species

Acanthosoma haemorrhoidale (page 22) is much larger and has red points to the projections on the pronotum and tip of the abdomen.

Elasmostethus interstinctus (page 26) is usually larger, has darker wing markings and lacks the distinctive pink-brown boomerang-shaped marking on the corium.

Pictures 1.and 2.adults in autumn

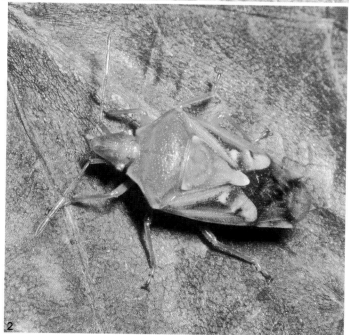

Acanthosomatidae

Elasmostethus interstinctus (Linnaeus, 1758)

Birch Shieldbug

ID features: A medium sized green bug, with dark red-brown and black markings on the corium.

Adult: August until June. They have been recorded at ivy blossom in late November.

Length: 8 to 11.5mm.

Larvae: Early June until early September, feeding on birch *Betula* spp., Hazel *Corylus avellana* and Aspen *Populus tremula*.

Habitat: A common woodland species that is also found in gardens, parks and mature hedgerows.

Distribution: Common and widely distributed throughout the British Isles.

Similar species

Acanthosoma haemorrhoidale (page 22) is much larger and has red points to the projections on the pronotum and tip of the abdomen.

Cyphostethus tristriatus (page 24) is on average smaller and has a pink-brown boomerang-shaped marking on the corium.

Pictures 1.and 3.two views of an adult, 2.early instar larva, 4.underside of an adult

Acanthosomatidae

Elasmucha grisea (Linnaeus, 1758)

Parent Bug

ID features: A medium sized bug with brown and orange markings on a blue-grey background and black markings on the connexivum.

Adult: August until early June, hibernating from late October. The male dies soon after emergence in early May.

Length: 7 to 9mm.

Larvae: Mid June until early August, feeding on birches *Betula* spp. The head, pronotum, scutellum and wing pads are a mustard yellow with black stripes running along them. The abdomen is bright green with a central yellow line and black marks on either side. The connexivum is yellow with small black ovals.

This species is so named, because of the parental care given by the female, who sits over the eggs for the two to three weeks until they hatch and then guards the newly hatched young. After the first moult the larvae follow the adult female. It is thought that the actions of the female may protect the larvae from predators and parasites, as she will place herself between any invader and her brood.

Habitat: Birch woods and also birch trees in parks and gardens.

Distribution: Common and widespread throughout most of the British Isles.

Similar species

This species is fairly distinct, although most similar to the mainly green *Elasmostethus interstinctus* (page 26), but the black markings on the connexivum and the blue-grey and orange markings on the head and pronotum, distinguishes *Elasmucha grisea* from other British shieldbugs.

Pictures 1.and 3.adult males, 2.female, 4.copulating pair with female on the right

Scutelleridae

Odontoscelis fuliginosa (Linnaeus, 1761)

ID features: This rounded bug has a dense covering of dark, red-brown hairs.

Adult: June and July.

Length: 6 to 8mm.

Larvae: Hibernation takes place as third or fourth instar larvae. Fifth instar larvae are found in the following May or June. They are thought to feed on stork's-bill *Erodium* spp., as they have been found under the leaves of that species and under adjacent mosses. The larvae are of a similar shape to the adult. They are brown, with black and yellow markings and a dark brown head. They are covered in punctures from which arise short dark hairs. The antennae and legs are dark brown, with strong spines on the tibia.

Habitat: In Britain this species is found on coastal sand dunes. It is a ground dweller amongst sparse vegetation, such as around rabbit warrens. It may also be found under stones, in sand or in patches of moss.

Distribution: Recorded in Kent and Pembrokeshire in recent times, although older records exist from many southern counties with sand dune systems. It is widespread in Europe, including inland sites.

Similar species

Odontoscelis lineola (page 32) has similar colour forms to *Odontoscelis fuliginosa*, but as well as the dark hairs, has several longitudinal bands of silver hairs over the pronotum and scutellum.

Pictures 1.and 3.two views of a mottled specimen, 2.streaked specimen

Scutelleridae

Odontoscelis lineola Rambur 1939

ID features: This species has dark hairs all over, with several bands of silver hairs running along the length of the pronotum and scutellum.

Adult: Usually recorded in June and July.

Length: 4 to 6mm.

Larvae: The larvae feed on the leaves of stork's-bill *Erodium* spp. They hibernate as third or fourth instar larvae. The parallel sided larvae are a dull black in colour and covered in long, rough hairs. The markings are indistinct, but similar to the adults. There are broad black markings around the connexivum.

Habitat: An inhabitant of coastal sand dunes and sandy heaths, burrowing around the base of the food plants and adjacent mosses.

Distribution: This species has a very local and scattered distribution in Britain. It is found in East Anglia, Surrey and Kent, as well as on other southern, coastal sand dunes. It is common in southern Europe.

Similar species

Odontoscelis fuliginosa (page 30) lacks the bands of silver hairs that *Odontoscelis lineola* has running along its length.

Pictures 1.and 2.two views of a streaked adult, 3.mottled adult

1

2

3

Scutelleridae

Eurygaster maura (Linnaeus, 1758)

ID features: The second segment of the antenna is nearly twice as long as the third. The central lobe of the head is level with the outer lobes at the apex and the inside edges of the outer lobes are nearly parallel. In the female the genital plates reach the sternum at their outer points. The colouring and intensity of the markings are variable.

Adult: August until late May.

Length: 8.5 to 10mm.

Larvae: Late May until August. The larvae are polyphagous on grasses (Poaceae) and cereals, but have also been recorded feeding on Common Knapweed *Centaurea nigra*. Late instar larvae are similar in shape and colouration to the adults. The early instars are darker with a pale central line down the pronotum.

Habitat: It prefers sunny grassy areas in Britain. It is a pest of cereal fields in parts of Europe.

Distribution: There are confirmed records from Kent, Surrey and Sussex. Many other records are due to confusion with the commoner *Eurygaster testudinaria*.

Similar species

Eurygaster testudinaria (page 36) is on average larger (9 to 11mm) than *Eurygaster maura*. It has the central lobe to the head depressed along its length compared with the outer lobes, while the outer lobes converge slightly towards their apex. The second segment of the antenna is only slightly longer than the third. In the female the genital plates do not reach the sternum at their outer points. The colour and intensity of the streaks vary.

(These characteristics are variable, but usable for identification in most cases. If in doubt the male genitalia may need to be checked for positive identification).

Pictures 1.and 2.views of an adult, 3.view of head showing lobes level at apex, 4.E.testudinaria showing depressed central lobe

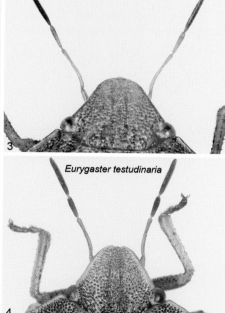

Eurygaster testudinaria

Scutelleridae

Eurygaster testudinaria (Geoffrey, 1785)

ID features: The central lobe of the head is depressed along its length compared with the outer lobes. The outer lobes converge slightly towards their apex. The second segment of the antenna is only slightly longer than the third. In the female the genital plates do not reach the sternum at their outer points. The colour and intensity of the streaks are variable.

Adult: Late July until June.

Length: 9 to 11mm.

Larvae: The larvae can be found from May until August feeding on rushes *Juncus* spp. and sedges *Carex* spp.

Habitat: A species of tall, damp grassland, especially within woods.

Distribution: Widespread although local in damp habitats across southern England, Wales and Ireland. In Britain it is much commoner and more widespread than *Eurygaster maura*.

Similar species

Eurygaster maura (page 34) is on average smaller (8.5 to 10mm). The second segment of the antenna is nearly twice as long as the third. The inside edges of the outer lobes of the head are nearly parallel and the central lobe is level with the outer lobes at the apex. In the female the genital plates reach the sternum at their outer points.

(These characteristics are variable, but usable for identification in most cases. If in doubt the male genitalia may need to be checked for positive identification).

Picture 1.pale adult, 2.well marked adult, 3.female genital plates, 4.late instar larva

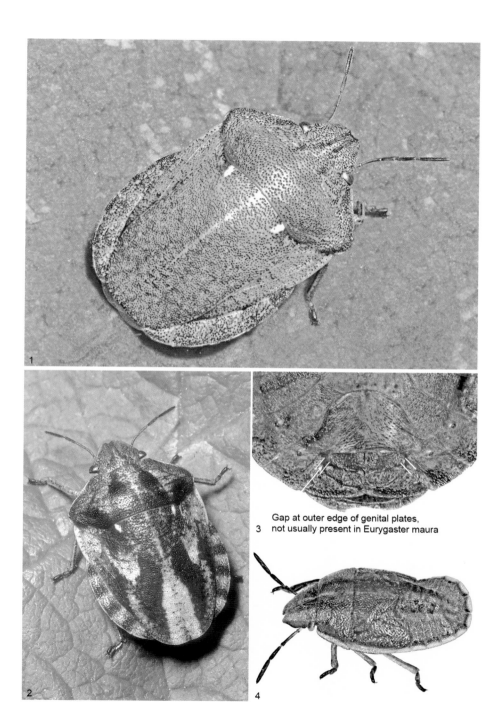

3   Gap at outer edge of genital plates,
not usually present in Eurygaster maura

Cydnidae

Legnotus limbosus (Geoffroy, 1785)

ID features: A small, rounded, black bug with a pale edge to the corium which reaches nearly as far back as the hemelytral membrane. It has a triangular shaped scutellum.

Adult: September until early June.

Length: 3.5 to 4.5mm.

Larvae: Late June until September, feeding on Lady's Bedstraw *Galium verum*, Goose-grass (Cleavers) *Galium aparine* and other bedstraws. The larvae have a shining black head and pronotum, with a bright red to pale pink abdomen, crossed by three or four black bands. There are black squares on the connexivum.

Habitat: Dry, south-facing grassy banks. It burrows into loose top soil at the base of the food plant.

Distribution: Southern and central England becoming scarce further north and west.

Similar species

Legnotus picipes (page 40) is black, of a similar size (3 to 4mm), but with the white edging to the corium only near the base.

Thyreocoris scarabaeoides (page 52) is all black and of a similar size (3 to 4mm). It lacks the white edge to the corium and the scutellum covers most of the abdomen.

Geotomus punctulatus (page 42) is black or black and red, of a similar size (3.5 to 4.5mm), with a few long hairs on the margins of the forewings, pronotum and head. It lacks the white edge to the corium.

Canthophorus impressus (page 46) is larger (6 to 7mm) and has a metallic green to violet sheen. There is a white margin to the pronotum as well as the corium.

Picture 1.adult showing extent of pale edge to corium, 2.adult, 3. head showing short central lobe

1

2

3

Cydnidae

Legnotus picipes (Fallen, 1807)

ID features: A black insect with a pale edge at the base of the corium. It has a triangular shaped scutellum.

Adult: Late July through to early July the following year.

Length: 3 to 4mm.

Larvae: June and July.

Habitat: A ground insect associated with various bedstraws *Galium* spp., growing on dry, well drained, sandy soils.

Distribution: Very local and possibly overlooked. In England it ranges from Hampshire west to Somerset, through Oxfordshire and on up to Humberside and most counties to the south and east of that.

Similar species

Legnotus limbosus (page 38) is slightly larger (3.5 to 4.5) with a pale edge to the corium reaching to about the hemelytral membrane, whereas *Legnotus picipes* has the white edge only at the base of the corium.

Thyreocoris scarabaeoides (page 52) is all black and of a similar size (3 to 4mm). It lacks the white edge to the base of the corium and the scutellum covers most of the abdomen.

Geotomus punctulatus (page 42) is black or black and red, of a similar size (3.5 to 4.5mm), with a few long hairs on the margins of the forewings, pronotum and head. It lacks the white edge to the base of the corium.

Canthophorus impressus (page 46) is larger (6 to 7mm) and often has a metallic green to violet sheen. The white margin edges the pronotum and all of the corium.

Picture 1.adult showing pale basal streak to corium, 2.dorsal view, 3.head showing almost equal length of lobes, 4 L.limbosus head showing shorter central lobe

1

2

3

4 *Legnotus limbosus*

Cydnidae

Geotomus punctulatus (Costa, 1847)

ID features: Mainly black, often with red markings on the corium and rear edge of the pronotum. It has a few long hairs on the margins of the head, pronotum and forewings.

Adult: August to early May.

Length: 3.5mm to 4.5mm.

Larvae: Late May and June. Appears to be associated with low growing Lady's Bedstraw *Galium verum*.

Habitat: A ground living bug found on or just beneath the surface of sand dunes, in small colonies of sparse vegetation.

Distribution: Recorded recently from only one site (Whitesand Bay) in West Cornwall. It has also been recorded in the past in South Wales. It is common in parts of southern Europe and the Channel Islands.

Similar species

Thyreocoris scarabaeoides (page 52) is all black and of a similar size (3 to 4mm). It is deeper in profile and lacks the long hairs on the margins of the head, pronotum and forewings.

Legnotus picipes (page 40) is black, of a similar size (3 to 4mm), but with a white edge to the base of the corium. It lacks the long hairs on the margins of the head, pronotum and forewings.

Legnotus limbosus (page 38) is black, of a similar size (3.5 to 4.5mm), with a pale edge to the corium. It lacks the long hairs on the margins of the head, pronotum and forewings.

Pictures 1.and 2.two views of the same adult

1

2

Cydnidae

Tritomegas (Sehirus) bicolor (Linnaeus, 1758)

Pied Shieldbug

ID features: A distinctive black and white species.

Adult: All year, with the adults first appearing in July and surviving until the following July. There may be two overlapping broods each summer.

Length: 5.5 to 7.5mm.

Larvae: May until late September, feeding on the seeds of White Dead-nettle *Lamium album*, Black Horehound *Ballota nigra* and possibly other Lamiaceae. The female exhibits brood care, laying her eggs in a hollow on the ground.

Habitat: A ground dwelling species that climbs the food plant to feed. In warm weather it will migrate and can at that time be found in trees. It is usually found along hedgerows, waste ground and woodland edges.

Distribution: Widespread in southern and central England and Wales, becoming scarce further north.

Similar species

A distinctive black and white species unlikely to be confused with any other British shieldbug, although the larvae are similar to those of *Eysarcoris fabricii* (page 62).

Pictures 1.and 2.adults showing distinctive pied markings, 3.and 4.last instar larvae

Cydnidae

Canthophorus (Sehirus) impressus Horvath, 1871

ID features: Metallic green, blue, violet or black with a white margin to the corium and pronotum.

Adult: August to June.

Length: 6 to 7mm.

Larvae: Mid May to July, feeding on Bastard Toadflax *Thesium humifusum*. The oval larvae are black in colour with a blue sheen over the head, pronotum, legs and antennae. The abdomen is red, marked with black in the centre and large black spots on the connexivum.

Habitat: This species is found on large stands of the food plant on short calcareous grassland with some bare ground. It hibernates communally in moss or under leaves.

Distribution: It is possibly declining in the southern counties of England. Wiltshire, Dorset and Oxfordshire appear to be the remaining stronghold for the species in Britain. It is widely distributed across Europe.

Similar species

Sehirus biguttatus (page 48) is slightly smaller (5 to 6.5mm) and has a pale spot in the corium.

Sehirus luctuosus (page 50) is larger (7 to 9mm) and lacks the pale margin to the corium and pronotum.

Pictures 1.and 2.two views of a blue adult

1

2

Cydnidae

Sehirus biguttatus (Linnaeus, 1758)

ID features: A blue-black bug with a pale margin to the corium and pronotum. It also has a pale spot in the corium.

Adult: August through until late spring.

Length: 5 to 6.5mm.

Larvae: June and July? They feed on Common Cow-wheat *Melampyrum pratense* and possibly Yellow Rattle *Rhinanthus minor*. The larvae are short and oval, with a brown to black head and pronotum and a reddish abdomen with square spots on the connexivum. The margins of the pronotum and wing pads are slightly paler.

Habitat: A ground-living species, found in the sunnier parts of woodland edge, rides and clearings on a wide variety of soils.

Distribution: A scarce and declining species, recorded locally in some southern and midland counties of England. There are a few older records from the north of England and Scotland.

Similar species

Canthophorus impressus (page 46) is slightly larger (6 to 7mm) and does not have the pale spot in the corium.

Pictures 1.and 2.two views of an adult

1

2

Cydnidae

Sehirus luctuosus Mulsant & Rey, 1866

ID features: A black species (sometimes with a bronze sheen).

Adult: Late July until late June.

Length: 7 to 9mm.

Larvae: Mid June until early August feeding on the leaves and seeds of Field Forget-me-not *Myosotis arvensis* and other *Myosotis* spp. The female exhibits brood care. The late instar larvae are of a similar shape and colour to the adults.

Habitat: A ground-living species, which will ascend the food plant to feed.

Distribution: Widespread in the south and midlands of England, becoming more scarce in the north and Wales.

Similar species

Canthophorus impressus (page 46) is smaller (6 to 7mm) and metallic blue-green (occasionally black) in colour. It has a pale edge to the corium and pronotum.

Sehirus biguttatus (page 48) is smaller (5 to 6.5mm), with a pale spot in the centre of the forewing and a pale edge to the corium and pronotum.

Zicrona caerulea (page 86) is smaller (5 to 7mm), but deeper in profile and has a blue-green overall sheen.

Pictures 1.to 3.three views of an adult

Thyreocoridae

Thyreocoris scarabaeoides (Linnaeus 1758)

Negro Bug

ID features: This bug is small and black with a slightly metallic blue/copper sheen. The scutellum covers most of the abdomen, rather than forming a triangular shape.

Adult: August until early June.

Length: 3 to 4mm.

Larvae: Late June until late August, feeding on *Viola* spp., including Hairy Violet *Viola hirta* and Field Pansy *Viola arvensis*. The larvae are oval and deep in profile. The head and pronotum are a bronze-black. The abdomen is white, with black punctures and bronze-black bars down the centre.

Habitat: Dry, south-facing grassy slopes, short turf and sandy areas. Predominantly coastal on sand dunes, although occasionally found inland on downland.

Distribution: Widespread in southern and central England and Wales, becoming more scarce further north, up to Lancashire. In Ireland recorded from the County Wexford sand dunes.

Similar species

Legnotus picipes (page 40) is black, of a similar size (3 to 4mm), but with a smaller triangular shaped scutellum and a white edge at the base of the corium.

Legnotus limbosus (page 38) is black, of a similar size (3.5 to 4.5mm), with a smaller triangular shaped scutellum and a pale edge to the corium.

Sehirus luctuosus (page 50) is much larger (7 to 9mm), with a proportionally smaller triangular shaped scutellum and is less deep in profile.

Geotomus punctulatus (page 42) is of a similar size (3.5 to 4.5mm), black or black and red, but shallower when viewed from the side, with a few long hairs on the margins of the forewings, pronotum and head.

Pictures 1.to 3.views of an adult

Pentatomidae

Podops inuncta (Fabricius, 1775)

ID features: This species has a large scutellum reaching the rear of the abdomen and has forward pointing projections on the pronotum at each side of the head.

Adult: August until June.

Length: 5.5 to 6mm.

Larvae: June until August. The food plant is unknown, but although this species has in the past been associated with dung and carrion they are most likely to feed on grasses. They are often found at the roots of plants. The oval larvae have a greyish-yellow head and pronotum, marked with black. The abdomen and wing pads are marked in red. The whole surface is covered in punctures. The legs are ochreous in colour.

Habitat: Usually found at ground level under stones or other objects in dry grassland, but is also found in damper grassland.

Distribution: Fairly common in southern and central England.

Similar species

Sciocoris cursitans (page 56) is a similar size (4.5 to 6mm), but is shallower in side profile, has a shorter scutellum and lacks the projections on the front of the pronotum on each side of the head.

Neottiglossa pusilla (page 60) is slightly smaller (4 to 4.5mm), with a much smaller triangular scutellum and without the projections at the front of the pronotum.

Pictures 1.to 4.four different adults, 2.clearly shows the projections on the front of the pronotum

Pentatomidae

Sciocoris cursitans (Fabricius, 1794)

ID features: This species is shallow in profile, with broad lateral extensions to the abdomen. The scutellum reaches just over half the length of the abdomen.

Adult: August until June. It is recorded as being able to stridulate loudly.

Length: 4.5 to 6mm.

Larvae: June until August. It appears to be associated with Mouse-eared Hawkweed *Pilosella officinarum* and *Potentilla* spp. The larvae are similar in colour and shape to the adult, but the abdomen has two pale, but prominent, transverse patches, which have black punctures on them with a black spot at each end.

Habitat: Dry, warm and sheltered slopes on calcareous grassland, or on sand. It is found on the ground amongst roots or amongst fine scree.

Distribution: A southern species recorded locally in most counties from Cornwall, up to Somerset and across to Kent and Essex.

Similar species

Podops inuncta (page 54) is deeper in profile, has a longer scutellum and has forward pointing projections on the front of the pronotum at each side of the head.

Neottiglossa pusilla (page 60) is slightly smaller (4 to 4.5mm), with an almost white edge to the pronotum, abdomen and the base of the corium.

Picture 1.adult, 2.and 3.different specimen

Pentatomidae

Aelia acuminata (Linnaeus, 1758)

Bishop's Mitre

ID features: A distinctive species with a pointed head and stripes along its length. It looks somewhat like a cereal grain.

Adult: August until June. Although it has been recorded in low numbers even in July.

Length: 8 to 9mm.

Larvae: June until August, feeding on the ripening seeds of a wide range of grasses (Poaceae).

Habitat: Tall and rank grassland, on road verges, field boundaries, woodland edge and along the coast. It hibernates amongst dead leaves, grass tufts and other dry places.

Distribution: Widespread and abundant in southern and central England and Wales, it becomes more scarce further north. It is an occasional pest of wheat in other parts of Europe.

Similar species

The distinctive shape and stripes along its length, distinguish this bug from all other British species of shieldbug.

The larvae of this species could be confused with the adults of *Neottiglossa pusilla* (page 60). The head of *N. pusilla* is short and triangular.

Pictures 1.and 4.adult, 2.early instar larva, 3.final instar larva

Pentatomidae

Neottiglossa pusilla (Gmelin, 1789)

ID features: Light brown in colour, with paler margins to the pronotum, abdomen and base of the corium. There is a pale central stripe down the pronotum and scutellum. It has a short triangular head.

Adult: Early August until early June. Hibernation starts in October.

Length: 4 to 4.5mm.

Larvae: July, feeding mainly on meadow-grasses *Poa* spp. The larvae are oval and strongly convex. The head and pronotum are ochreous and have black punctures and black margins. There are two zigzag lines running from the central lobe of the face. The abdomen is pale yellow with black punctures, black dorsal bands and black markings on the connexivum. The legs are similar in colour and markings to the adults.

Habitat: Damp grassland.

Distribution: An often scarce, but widely distributed species in southern England, between Norfolk and Cornwall. It is widespread throughout Europe.

Similar species

Aelia acuminata (page 58) larvae could be confused with the adults of this species. The head of *Aelia acuminata* is elongate and narrow at the front. *Neottiglossa pusilla* has a shorter broader head.

Pictures 1.to 4.four views of an adult

2

3

4

Pentatomidae

Eysarcoris fabricii (Kirkaldy 1904)

ID features: The head, front of the pronotum and the patch at the base of the scutellum are all a metallic magenta, with a green to bronze sheen.

Adult: August until early July.

Length: 5 to 7mm.

Larvae: Late June until as late as October, forming a colony feeding on the seeds of Hedge Woundwort *Stachys sylvatica* and sometimes White Dead-nettle *Lamium album*.

Habitat: Hedgerows, wasteland and woodland edges.

Distribution: Common and widespread in southern and central England and Wales. This species was rare at the end of the 19th century, but has since expanded its range.

Similar species

Eysarcoris aeneus (page 64) lacks the dark metallic blotch on the scutellum, but has a distinct pale spot in each of the basal corners of that area.

Pictures 1.and 2.well marked adult, 3.copulating pair, 4.early instar larva in seed head of Stachys sylvatica, *5.final instar larva*

Pentatomidae

Eysarcoris aeneus (Scopoli, 1763)

ID features: A dark yellow-brown species, with a pale spot at the basal angles of the scutellum.

Adult: September until June.

Length: 5 to 6mm.

Larvae: July and August. The larvae are colonial, feeding on the fruits of Slender St. John's-wort *Hypericum pulchrum*. The larvae are short, broad, and very convex, with large areas of black punctuation. They have a large head and a trapezoidal pronotum.

Habitat: Damp heathland and acid grassland and in clearings and rides in woodland. Over wintering takes place in moss or in the soil.

Distribution: This bug is reasonably well established only in the New Forest, Hampshire with isolated reports from Wales and some southern and midland counties. It is scarce, but possibly overlooked. It is widely distributed on the continent.

Similar species

Eysarcoris fabricii (page 62) has a large bronze spot in the centre of the scutellum, but lacks the pale spots in the basal angles of that area.

Pictures 1.and 2.side and dorsal views of an adult

Pentatomidae

Palomena prasina (Linnaeus, 1761)

Green Shieldbug

ID features: A large green bug with dark wing-tips and slight lateral extension to the pronotum. The last two segments of the antennae are reddish in colour. The bug becomes a dark reddish-brown in winter, returning to green again in the spring.

Adult: Mainly September until July. Although it has also been recorded in August.

Length: 12 to 13.5mm.

Larvae: June until early October, feeding on a large variety of native and alien broad-leaved trees and shrubs.

Habitat: Woodlands, hedgerows, parks, gardens and waste ground .

Distribution: Very common and widespread in southern and central England, Wales and Ireland, becoming more scarce further north.

Similar species

Piezodorus lituratus (page 72) The colour of this species in spring is yellow-green, with a yellow edge all round. It has pinkish-red antennae and pale blue edges to the corium. The pronotum is not laterally extended as in *Palomena prasina*.

Nezara viridula (page 68) is a rare, newly naturalised species, that is nearly all green in colour, without any dark punctures and three to five pale markings at the base of the scutellum.

Picture 1.summer adult, 2.winter adult, 3.larva, 4.larvae hatching, 5.final instar larva

66

Pentatomidae

Nezara viridula (Linnaeus 1758)

Southern Green Shieldbug

ID features: A large green shieldbug without dark punctures. It has 3 to 5 light spots on the front of the scutellum and a dark spot in the basal corners. There is a low conical area near the outer edge of the pronotum. Southern European forms are edged with pale brown.

Adult: The extent of the adult stage in Britain is not yet established, although it appears to overwinter. Individual specimens arrived in the past as assisted aliens, imported with vegetables into the British Isles, but were thought to be unable to survive the winter climate until recently.

Length: 11 to 15mm.

Larvae: The recent colonists have been recorded in August (5th instar) and September, on a wide range of plants including Tomato *Lycopersicum esculentum*, *Viburnum* spp., goldenrod *Solidago* spp. and Hemp Agrimony *Eupatorium cannabinum* (Brooke, Sheila E. 2004). The early instar larvae are black with four rows of white spots down the abdomen and red margins to the pronotum. Late instar larvae are green, with four rows of white spots, plus red markings edging the abdomen, as well as the red margins to the pronotum.

Habitat: Gardens and an urban nature reserve at present, but it may spread to other habitats if the colonisation continues.

Distribution: This is a very recent colonist in Britain, colonies were recorded in the Queens Park area and in the Kings Cross area of North London in 2003 (Barclay, M.V.L., 2004) and (Shardlow, M.E.A. & Taylor, R. 2004).

Similar species

Palomena prasina (page 66) has a more laterally extended pronotum. The punctures in this species are dark, giving a finely black dotted appearance.

Piezodorus lituratus (page 72) The colour of this species in spring is yellow-green, but with a yellow edge all round. It also has dark punctures, pinkish-red antennae and a pale blue edge to the corium.

Pictures 1.and 2.adult of all green form

1

2

Pentatomidae

Dolycoris baccarum (Linnaeus, 1758)

Sloe Bug

ID features: This species has purplish-brown forewings, a yellowish pronotum and scutellum and a yellow connexivum with black markings. It is covered in long hairs, which can be seen most easily on the pronotum and legs. It becomes an overall dull brown in winter.

Adult: August until early July.

Length: 11 to 12mm.

Larvae: July to September, feeding on the flowers and occasionally the fruit of a wide variety of plants, especially Blackthorn *Prunus spinosa*, Damson *Prunus insitia* and other Rosaceae.

Habitat: Tall vegetation and shrubs in hedgerows and along the edge of woodland.

Distribution: Common and widespread throughout Britain, but becoming more scarce in northern Scotland.

Similar species

Holcostethus vernalis (page 108) is a rare migrant, which is smaller (9.5 to 11mm) and is not hairy.

Piezodorus lituratus (page 72) in its sexually immature late summer form, is similar in size (10 to 13mm), but has a broad blue margin to the corium and a red band across the rear of the pronotum.

Pictures 1.and 3.summer adults, 2.winter adult, 4.early instar larva, 5.final instar larva

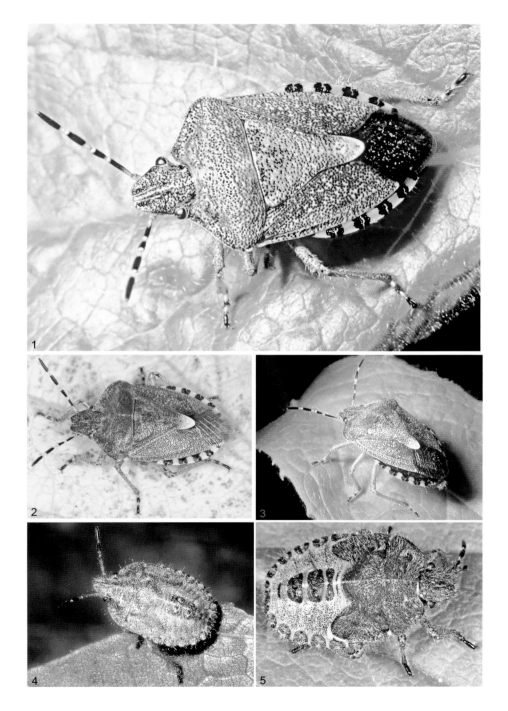

Pentatomidae

Piezodorus lituratus (Fabricius, 1794)

Gorse Shieldbug

ID features: The sexually immature late summer adults, have purplish-red markings at the rear of the pronotum and on the corium, but when they emerge from hibernation in the spring they are mainly yellow-green. As with the late summer adults, these have pink antennae and blue edges to the corium.

Adult: Late July until early June.

Length: 10 to 13mm.

Larvae: June until early August, feeding on the seed-pods of gorse *Ulex* spp., Broom *Cytisus scoparius*, Dyer's Green-weed *Genista tinctoria* and occasionally other plants in the family Genisteae. They have also been recorded on Laburnum *Laburnum anagyroides* and clovers *Trifolium* spp.

Habitat: Commons, heaths, parks and gardens.

Distribution: Widespread across Britain and Ireland wherever the food plants are present.

Similar species

Palomena prasina (page 66) is greener and lacks the all pink antennae, yellow edging to the abdomen and grey-blue edges to the corium. It also has lateral extensions to the pronotum.

Pitedia juniperina (page 109) is bright green rather than yellow-green and has a much broader pale margin to the lateral edges of the pronotum.

Nezara viridulis (page 68) is a rare, newly naturalised species, that is on average larger (11 to 15mm) than *P.lituratus* and nearly all green in colour.

Picture 1.spring adult, 2.late instar larva, 3.adult showing abdominal projection between hind legs, 4.late summer adult

Pentatomidae

Pentatoma rufipes (Linnaeus, 1758)

Forest Bug

ID features: A large brown shieldbug with orange legs and a noticeable orange or yellow tip to the triangular scutellum. The pronotum has raised and rounded lateral extensions.

Adult: July to November. Adults have occasionally been recorded in April and May.

Length: 11 to 14mm.

Larvae: August until July (over-wintering as a larva). The larvae feed on oak *Quercus* spp. and to a lesser extent on Alder *Alnus glutinosa* and other native trees and shrubs. They also feed on cultivated trees such as apple *Malus* spp. and cherry *Prunus* spp.

Habitat: Mostly in oak woods, but also in orchards and gardens.

Distribution: Widespread throughout Britain.

Similar species

Troilus luridus (page 82) has a yellow band on the last but one segment of the antennae. It also lacks the orange tip to the scutellum and the orange legs.

Picromerus bidens (page 80) has thorn-like projections on the pronotum.

Pictures 1.and 2.views of typical adult, 3.late instar larva (April), 4.drab coloured adult

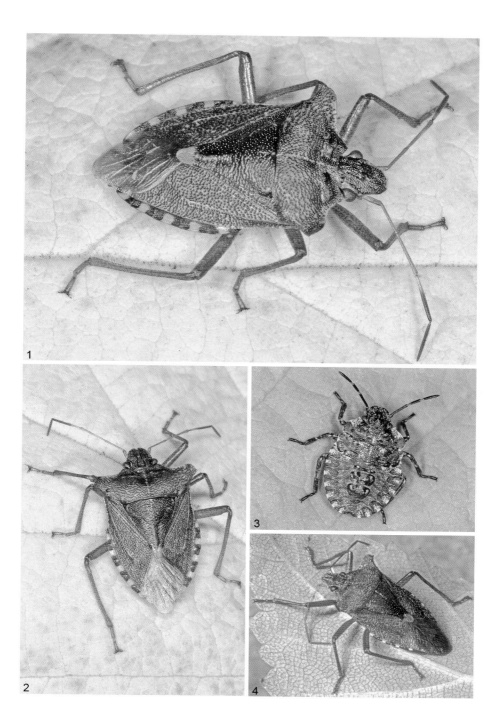

1

2

3

4

Pentatomidae

Eurydema oleracea (Linnaeus, 1758)

Brassica Bug

ID features: There are many colour forms. The usual colour is a metallic green, but this can be blue, black or violet. These colours are overlain with red, yellow, cream or orange spots.

Adult: Late July to May.

Length: 6 to 7mm.

Larvae: Late May until July, feeding on members of the cabbage family (Brassicaceae), including Horse-radish *Armoracia rusticana* and cultivated species. They may also be found on members of the carrot family (Apiaceae). The larvae are similar in shape to the adults. The wing pads are black and the abdomen is pale yellow with central black bands and prominent black rectangles on the connexivum.

Habitat: It can be found on woodland edge, wasteland, farmland and gardens, wherever suitable plants are present.

Distribution: A scarce species in southern England, as far north as Gloucestershire across to Cambridgeshire.

Similar species

Eurydema dominulus (page 78) usually has a red ground colour overlain with black, whereas *Eurydema oleracea* is dark with a metallic sheen, overlain with shades of red or cream.

Pictures 1.and 3.pale form of adult, 2.red form

1

2   3

Pentatomidae

Eurydema dominulus (Scopoli, 1763)

ID features: This species is usually red overlain with black markings, but colours can be variable.

Adult: August to May, over-wintering under bark and in leaf litter.

Length: 6 to 7mm.

Larvae: June until August, feeding on Lady's Smock *Cardamine pratensis,* Lesser Swine-cress *Coronopus didymus* and other members of the cabbage family (Brassicaceae), including cultivated plants. The larvae are similar in shape to the adult with an orange ground colour. The head, antennae and legs are black and there are two large black patches on the pronotum. The scutellum and wing pads are also black, but the outer margins of the wing pads are orange.

Habitat: Woodland rides and clearings where the adults can be found feeding on blossoms.

Distribution: It is a scarce insect in Britain, found in Kent and Sussex with old, occasional records from other southern counties. It is a common and serious agricultural pest on the continent.

Similar species

Eurydema oleracea (page 76) is dark and metallic overlain with shades of red or cream, whereas the ground colour of *Eurydema dominulus* is red overlain with black.

There are several other red and black *Eurydema* spp. elsewhere in Europe that may become occasional migrants. These are all more than 7mm in length.

Pictures 1.and 2.adult

Pentatomidae

Picromerus bidens (Linnaeus, 1758)

ID features: A brown shieldbug with large thorn-like extensions to the pronotum.

Adult: July until November.

Length: 12 to 13.5mm.

Larvae: Mid-May until late August, feeding as predators of moth, butterfly (Lepidoptera) and leaf beetle larvae (Coleoptera), although they will also take the sap of plants. The eggs are laid between late August and early October and although these bugs normally over-winter in the egg stage, they may also over-winter as larvae. The larvae are rounder than the adults. They are grey and black with distinctive black and yellow antennae and legs.

Habitat: The usual habitat is lush vegetation, at warm, sheltered sites by water margins, woodland edges or similar places.

Distribution: Common and widespread in southern and central England, Wales and Ireland, becoming less common further north.

Note: On the continent, *P. bidens* has been used as a biological control for pine moths, as well as for other insects in greenhouses. It has also been used, less successfully, to combat Colorado Beetle *Leptinotarsa decemlineata*.

Similar species

Both *Pentatoma rufipes* (page 74) and *Troilus luridus* (page 82) lack the thorn-like projections on the pronotum.

Pictures 1.to 3.views of an adult

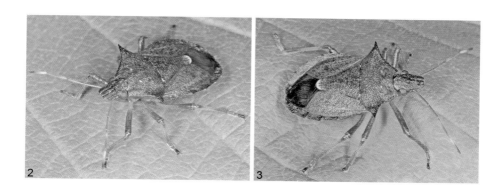

Pentatomidae

Troilus luridus (Fabricius, 1775)

ID features: This shieldbug has an orange-yellow band on the last but one segment of its antennae. It lacks an orange tip to the scutellum and has mottled brown legs.

Adult: July until June.

Length: 10 to 12mm.

Larvae: June until September, feeding on plants while young, but preying on the larvae of moths (Lepidoptera) and beetles (Coleoptera), as they become larger.

Habitat: A woodland species, occurring at all heights amongst the foliage of coniferous and broad-leaved trees and shrubs.

Distribution: Widespread across southern and central England and Wales as far north as Durham. It is also present throughout most of Ireland.

Similar species

Picromerus bidens (page 80) has pointed thorn-like projections on the pronotum.

Pentatoma rufipes (page 74) lacks the yellow band on the last but one segment of the antennae. It has an orange tip to the scutellum and has orange legs.

Pictures 1.and 3.adult, 2.and 4.final instar larva

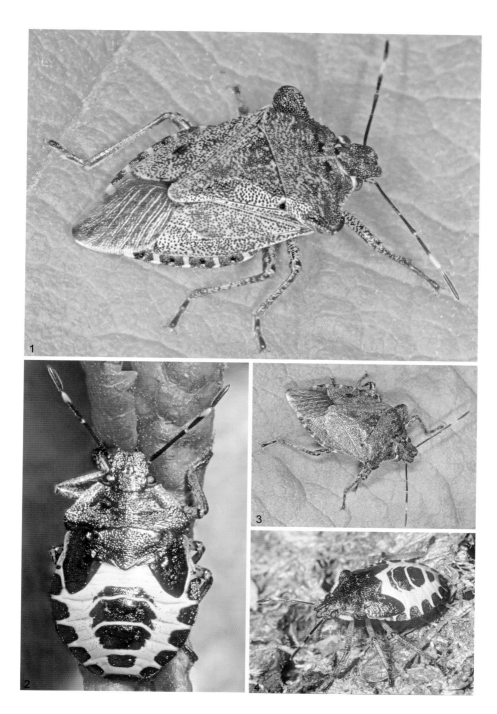

Pentatomidae

Rhacognathus punctatus (Linnaeus, 1758)

Heather Bug

ID features: This bug is variable in colour, but is generally a metallic blue-green to bronze over an orange-red background, with an orange or red mid line on the pronotum and orange-red bands across the legs.

Adult: August to June.

Length: 7 to 9mm.

Larvae: June to August, predating the Heather Beetle *Lochmaea suturalis* and also other Coleoptera, including the closely related *Lochmaea capreae* which is found on stunted sallows *Salix* spp.

Habitat: It is found sparingly on heaths, in damper areas amongst Sphagnum moss or in mixed vegetation at the margins.

Distribution: Throughout Britain in suitable habitats.

Similar species

Although there is a variation in how metallic these insects appear, the banded legs and orange-red line down the centre of the pronotum should distinguish this bug from other British shieldbugs.

Pictures 1.and 2.strongly metallic form, 3.brown form

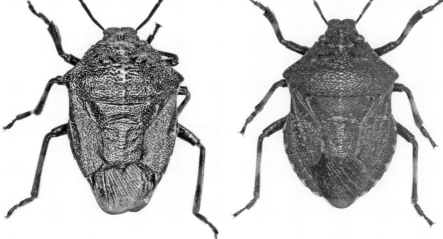

1

2

3

Pentatomidae

Zicrona caerulea (Linnaeus, 1758)

Blue Bug

ID features: A dark, medium sized shieldbug with a blue-green overall sheen and a dark hemelytral membrane.

Adult: July until June.

Length: 5 to 7mm.

Larvae: June and July. They are predators on leaf beetle larvae (Chrysomelidae) and moth and butterfly larvae (Lepidoptera).

Habitat: Sites and habitats which support abundant populations of the larger leaf beetle species: including heaths, marshes, calcareous grasslands and woodland rides.

Distribution: Widespread in suitable habitats throughout Britain, especially in the north where it can be abundant.

Similar species

Thyreocoris scarabaeoides (page 52) is smaller (3 to 4mm) and black with a slightly metallic blue/copper sheen, but has the scutellum covering most of the abdomen.

Canthophorus impressus (page 46) is of a similar size (6 to 7mm) and metallic blue-green, but with a pale edge to the corium and pronotum.

Sehirus luctuosus (page 50) is larger (7 to 9mm), less deep in side profile and lacks the blue sheen.

Pictures 1.and 2.adult, 3.adult, 4.late instar larva

1

2

3

4

Coreidae

Gonocerus acuteangulatus (Goeze, 1778)

Box Bug

ID features: A relatively large, reddish-brown species with a narrow abdomen and pointed extremities to the pronotum.

Adult: Mid August until July.

Length: 11 to 14mm.

Larvae: July until September. Although the larvae have been associated with Box *Buxus sempervirens* in Britain, they are probably feeding on the fruit and seeds of a variety of trees and shrubs. They have been beaten from Hawthorn *Crataegus monogyna* as both adults and larvae and have also been found on other plants. In parts of the Mediterranean it can be a pest on Hazel *Corylus avellana*. Continental bugs are also known to feed on oak *Quercus* spp., alder *Alnus* spp. and buckthorn *Rhamnus* spp.. The larvae have a narrow, reddish brown head and pronotum, with a wider, more oval abdomen. The abdomen is bright green with a yellow edge to the connexivum. There are scattered tubercles (bumps) over the whole of the upper surface.

Habitat: Bushes, hedgerows and small trees on downland. It may now be expanding into other habitats.

Distribution: Traditionally known only from Box Hill in Surrey, but it appears to be expanding its range and food plants. In the 1990's it was found to have spread over 10km from Box Hill on to the surrounding downs and commons. In 2002 it was found in the Brighton area of Sussex. It has since been recorded again in Sussex and also Hampshire and Berkshire. In August 2003, one was found on the pavement outside of the Bristol City Museum and Art Gallery, over 150km to the west of its core range.

Similar species

Coreus marginatus (page 90) is slightly larger (13 to 15mm) and broader across the abdomen. It lacks the pointed lateral extremities to the pronotum.

Enoplops scapha (page 94) has a broader abdomen and is much darker in colour. It also lacks the pointed lateral extremities to the pronotum.

Pictures 1.and 2.adult found in Bristol

Coreidae

Coreus marginatus (Linnaeus, 1758)

ID features: A large, mottled brown bug with a broad abdomen.

Adult: August through to July.

Length: 13 to 15mm.

Larvae: July until September feeding on the leaves and ripening seeds of plants in the dock family (Polygonaceae), ranging from sorrels *Rumex* spp. to Rhubarb *Rheum rhabarbarum.*

Habitat: A wide variety of habitats, but particularly in dense vegetation along hedgerows, wasteland and damper areas.

Distribution: Common and widespread in southern England, Wales and Ireland, becoming more scarce further north.

Similar species

Enoplops scapha (page 94) is usually darker in colour, is narrower across the pronotum and has contrasting creamy-yellow markings on the connexivum.

Gonocerus acuteangulatus (page 88) has a narrower abdomen and is usually lighter in colour. It has pointed lateral extremities to the pronotum.

Syromastes rhombeus (page 92) has a broader distinctly diamond shaped abdomen.

Picture 1.and 3.adults, 2.larva

Coreidae

*Syromastes (**Verlusia**) rhombeus* (Linnaeus, 1767)

ID features: The abdomen of this bug is very broad and diamond-shaped.

Adult: Late August, over wintering as an adult and appearing again in May. It hibernates at the base of trees or in grass tufts.

Length: 9.5 to 10.5mm.

Larvae: June to August feeding on various spurreys *Spergularia* spp. and sandworts *Arenaria* spp. The final instar larvae are similar to the adults in both shape and colour and the whole of their upper surface is covered in white hairy tubercles. The tergites (dorsal plates of the abdomen) are angled at the margins and have a strong spine on them. The scent glands are orange in colour and also have a stout spine in front of them.

Habitat: A sandy heathland and grassland species. It can also be found in chalk and sand pits.

Distribution: A coastal species in southern England, from South Wales across to Suffolk.

Similar species

Coreus marginatus (page 90) is a larger bug (13 to 15mm), with a less laterally extended abdomen, which is oval rather than diamond-shaped.

Enoplops scapha (page 94) is larger (11 to 12mm), usually darker in colour, is narrower across the abdomen and has contrasting creamy-yellow markings on the connexivum.

Gonocerus acuteangulatus (page 88) is larger (11 to 14mm), has a narrower abdomen and has more pointed lateral extremities to the pronotum.

Pictures 1.and 2.two views of the same adult, 3.different adult

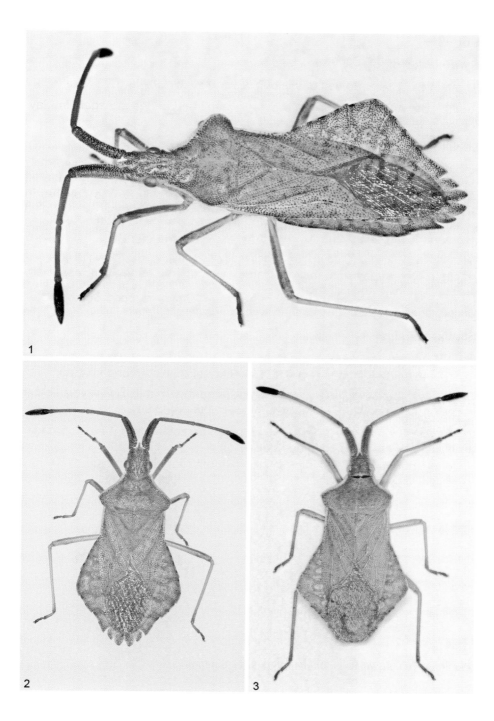

Coreidae

Enoplops scapha (Fabricius, 1794)

ID features: This species is usually dark grey in colour, with contrasting creamy-yellow markings on the connexivum.

Adult: Late July until late June.

Length: 11 to 12mm.

Larvae: From late May until August, feeding on plants in the daisy family (Compositae). It is recorded as preferring Scentless Mayweed *Tripleurospermum maritimum* as a food plant. The head and pronotum are brown to black, the abdomen pale green with a scalloped edge. In the centre there is a brown patch, with two erect spines on the adjoining segment. The larvae are covered in hairs and have very long, thick, spiny antennae, which are especially noticeable in the earlier instars.

Habitat: Dry, sunny and sheltered areas with sparse vegetation, especially coastal sandhills and cliff faces.

Distribution: Southern coasts from Kent to Pembrokeshire.

Similar species

Coreus marginatus (page 90) is larger (13 to 15mm), is usually mottled, paler brown and is broader across the pronotum.

Gonocerus acuteangulatus (page 88) has a narrower abdomen and is lighter in colour. It has pointed lateral extremities to the pronotum.

Syromastes rhombeus (page 92) is paler in colour and has a broader distinctly diamond-shaped abdomen.

Pictures 1.to 3.adults

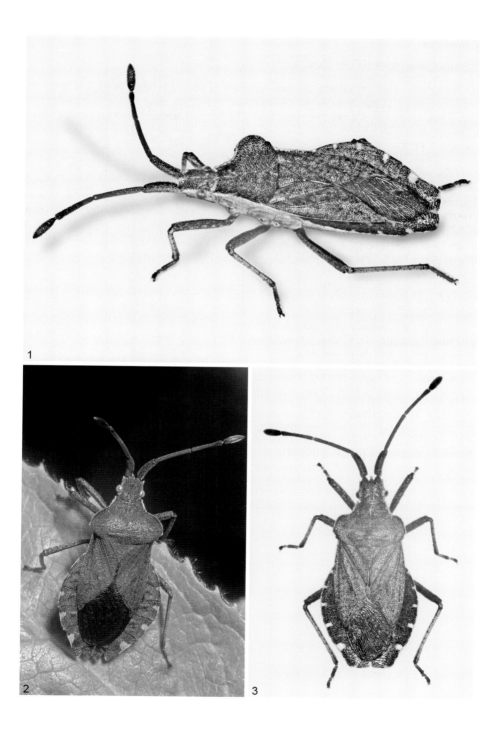

1
2
3

Coreidae

Spathocera dahlmanni (Schilling, 1829)

ID features: The pronotum of this species is much longer than it is wide. It has a distinct black quarter circle marked on each side of the scutellum. It lacks the long spines on the pronotum, head and antennae that are present in the *Arenocoris* spp.

Adult: Mid August until May or June.

Length: 5 to 6.5mm.

Larvae: July until September, feeding on the stems of Sheep's Sorrel *Rumex acetosella*. The larvae are of a similar shape to the adults. They have a dark yellowish head and a red pronotum. The abdomen is yellow, with a tinge of red. There is a scattering of tubercles over the whole upper surface. They have two very prominent red scent glands and yellow legs and antennae.

Habitat: Dry, warm, sandy places on acid soil, with sparse vegetation where *Rumex acetosella* grows. The adults feed on the seeds. The species prefers recently burnt areas, or areas around rabbit warrens, where there are very degraded plants. The communal hibernation often takes place amongst pine *Pinus* spp. debris or in grass tufts.

Distribution: Found in southern England, particularly on the heaths of Surrey, Hampshire and Dorset. It has recently been recorded in Berkshire. It is widely distributed in Europe.

Similar species

Arenocoris falleni (page 100) and *Arenocoris waltli* (page 102) are spiny on the pronotum, head and antennae and the pronotum is wider than it is long.

Bathysolen nubilus (page 98) also has a pronotum that is wider than it is long and has more protruding eyes than *Spathocera dahlmanni.*

Pictures 1.to 4. adult on its food plant

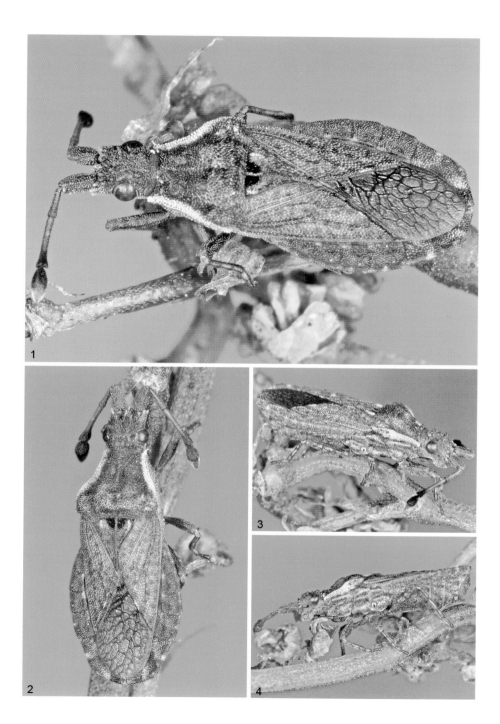

Coreidae

Bathysolen nubilus (Fallén, 1807)

ID features: This species lacks the long spines on the pronotum, head and antennae that are present in the *Arenocoris* spp., although there is a large spine near the apex of the rear femur. It has very pale and slightly inrolled forward margins to the pronotum. The tip of the scutellum is also pale.

Adult: Late July until mid June.

Length: 5.5 to 7mm.

Larvae: June and July on stunted plants of Black Medick *Medicago lupulina*, Tall Melilot *Melilotus altissima* and probably other plants in the pea family (Fabaceae).

Habitat: Sparse vegetation on bare, dry ground, including coastal shingle, waste ground, quarries and gravel pits. The bug hibernates as an adult under stones or earth, or amongst grasses, mosses and dead leaves.

Distribution: A scarce species in Britain, that is possibly expanding its range. It is found in south-eastern England, especially Kent, but also in East Anglia and the counties around London. It is widespread in Europe.

Similar species

Arenocoris falleni (page 100) has long spines on the pronotum, head and antennae, but does not have a large spine near the apex of the rear femur.

Arenocoris waltli (page 102) has long spines on the pronotum, head and antennae. It lacks the pale and slightly inrolled forward margins to the pronotum and the pale tip to the scutellum.

Spathocera dahlmanni (page 96) has a pronotum that is much longer than it is wide. The pronotum in *Bathysolen nubilus* is much wider than it is long. *Spathocera dahlmanni* also has large, but much less protruding eyes and has a pale tip to the scutellum.

Pictures 1.and 2.adult

2

Coreidae

Arenocoris falleni (Schilling, 1829)

ID features: The last but one segment to the antenna is pale and parallel sided. There are two rows of spines on the pronotum that form a 'V' shape. There are no large spines near the apex of the rear femur.

Adult: July until May, but possibly double brooded in favourable conditions so could be found as an adult at any time.

Length: 6 to 7mm.

Larvae: June and July feeding on stork's-bill *Erodium* spp. They are pale ochreous in colour with a tinge of pink.

Habitat: Found on evolved sand dunes where its food plant is present. It over winters under stones or in grass tufts.

Distribution: A coastal species recorded from Norfolk around the south coast of England, up to the south coast of Wales. It is widespread in Europe, where it is not confined to the coast.

Similar species

Arenocoris waltli (page102) has a large spine near the apex of the rear femur. The last, but one segment to the antenna becomes wider and darkens towards its apex. The spines on the pronotum are randomly placed and not in two distinct rows.

Bathysolen nubilus (page 98) has pale and slightly inrolled forward margins to the pronotum. The rear femur has a large spine near the apex.

Spathocera dahlmanni (page 96) has a distinct black quarter circle marked on each side of the scutellum and the pronotum is much longer than it is wide. The pronotum in *Arenocoris falleni* is wider than it is long.

Pictures 1.and 2.adult

Coreidae

Arenocoris waltli (Herrich-Schäffer, 1834)

ID features: This species has a large spine near the apex of the rear femur. The last but one segment of the antenna becomes wider and darkens towards its apex. The spines on the pronotum are randomly placed and not in two distinct rows.

Adult: August to May.

Length: 7 to 7.5mm.

Larvae: The food plant is probably stork's-bill *Erodium* spp. Early stages appear to be unrecorded in Britain.

Habitat: Sparse vegetation and bare ground in sandy areas and dunes.

Distribution: The Breckland areas of Norfolk and Suffolk are the only British sites. The last recorded specimen was collected in 1964 (it was recently discovered in the collections of the National Museum of Wales, Cardiff). The last record previous to that was in 1935, but the species may still be present in low numbers.

Similar species:

Arenocoris falleni (page 100) has no large spine near the apex of the rear femur. The last, but one segment to the antenna is pale and parallel sided. There are two rows of spines on the pronotum that form a 'V' shape.

Bathysolen nubilus (page 98) has very pale and slightly inrolled forward margins to the pronotum. The tip of the scutellum is also pale. This species lacks the long spines on the pronotum, head and antennae that are present in the *Arenocoris* spp.

Spathocera dahlmanni (page 96) has a distinct black quarter circle marked on each side of the scutellum and the pronotum is much longer than it is wide. The pronotum in *Arenocoris waltli* is wider than it is long.

Pictures 1.and 2.adult

1

2

Coreidae

Ceraleptus lividus Stein, 1858

ID features: This species has yellow sides to the head with a black eye stripe. It also has a creamy-white basal stripe to the corium.

Adult: August to June. Possibly two generations in some years.

Length: 9 to 11mm.

Larvae: Late June to early August feeding on Red Clover *Trifolium pratense* and other *Trifolium* and *Lotus* spp.

Habitat: On dry soils in places such as commons, sand dunes and gravel pits. It over winters under bark and also in moss, dead leaves and grass tussocks.

Distribution: South-east England, inland as far as Surrey and Bedfordshire. A scarce species, that is possibly under recorded.

Similar species

This comparitively large species lacks the laterally extended pronotum, or the spines of the other British Coreidae. For this reason it is fairly easy to identify. If there is any difficulty, the yellow sides to the head, the black eye stripe and the creamy-white edge to the base of the corium can be used for a positive identification.

Pictures 1.and 2.adult

1

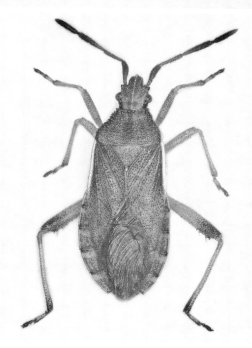

2

Coreidae

Coriomeris denticulatus (Scopoli, 1763)

ID features: A slender bug, with a white spiny margin to the pronotum and base of the corium. The spines on the pronotum each ending in a dark bristle. Most surfaces of the bug, especially the antennae and legs are also covered in bristles.

Adult: August to June.

Length: 7 to 9mm.

Larvae: The larva feed from late June until August on Black Medick *Medicago lupulina*, melilots *Melilotus* spp. and probably clovers *Trifolium* spp.

Habitat: Dry, sheltered, sunny banks on calcareous grassland, sheltered embankments and in gravel pits.

Distribution: Southern and central England and Wales. It is scarce further north.

Similar species

The spiny white margin to the pronotum and corium and the numerous bristles elsewhere, distinguish this insect from all other British Coreidae.

Pictures 1.adult, 2.and 3.two views of another specimen, 4.third adult

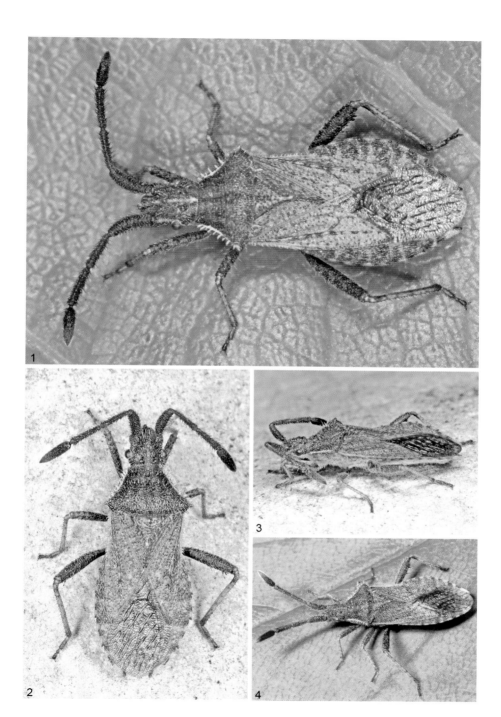

Migrants, vagrants and former residents

Acanthosomatidae

Elasmucha ferrugata (Fabricius, 1787) **Bilberry Shieldbug** This is a large red-brown bug that has a broad pronotum with thorn-like extremities. There are 4 old records from the Midlands of England. It was last recorded in 1950, but because of its habitat it may since have been overlooked. The food plants are Bilberry *Vaccinum myrtillus* and Cowberry *Vaccinum vitis-idaea*.

Scutelleridae

Eurygaster austriaca (Schrank, 1776)   Slightly larger than the native *Eurygaster* spp. (page 34 to 36). It has a keel along the scutellum and the outer lobes of the head meet at the snout, giving the central lobe a diamond-shaped appearance. It probably bred on the Kent coast in Victorian times, but is not thought to have done so since. It was also recorded in the New Forest in the first part of the 20th Century. This species is on the edge of its range in Britain, but could recolonise. The food plants are grasses and cereals (Poaceae).

Cydnidae

Cydnus aterrimus (Forster, 1771)   A flattened blue-black bug, which is at first glance similar to *Geotomus punctulatus* (page 42), but with a narrower head, smaller scutellum and pale hemelytral membrane. The bug has a semicircular rear margin to the corium. It is recorded from the Channel Islands, is widespread in Europe and is found under spurges *Euphorbia* spp.

Byrsinus (Aethus) flavicornis (Fabricius, 1794)   This small (2.5 to 3.5mm) brown to black species, has spiny legs and margins to the head. It also has hairs on the margins of the pronotum and abdomen. It was recorded on the Isle of Wight in 1895, but more recently on the Channel Islands, on thyme *Thymus* spp. and restharrow *Ononis* spp., in hot sandy places on dunes.

Pentatomidae

Jalla dumosa (Linnaeus, 1758) This (11 to 15mm) brown species is similar to, but larger than *Rhacognathus punctatus* (page 84). It has a pale band across the tibia, a longitudinal pale stripe from the head to the scutellum, pale front margins to the pronotum and a pale spot in each of the basal angles of the scutellum. It was recorded (including a larva) on coastal sand dunes in east Kent during the late 19th Century. It is predacious on the larvae of Lepidoptera.

Holcostethus vernalis (Wolff, 1804)   A medium sized (9.5 to 10.5mm) yellow-brown insect. It looks similar to *Dolycoris baccarum* (page 70), but lacks the covering of hairs and has pale lateral edges to the pronotum. The second and third segments of the antenna are orange without the black median bands found in *D.baccarum*. There have been occasional scattered records from southern and central England, especially in Kent where it may have bred. There was an East Sussex record in 2003. It is common in much of Europe. The species has been taken from a wide range of trees, shrubs and herbaceous plants. It may be partially predacious.

Dyroderes umbraculatus (Fabricius, 1775)   A medium-sized species (8mm), with a rounded abdomen and white patches on the 'shoulders' of the pronotum. It is recorded from the Channel Islands on bedstraws *Galium* spp.

Eurydema ornatum (Linnaeus, 1758)   One of several red bugs that are similar to *Eurydema dominulus* (page 78). It is larger with a dark marking along the margin of the corium. This species may appear on the British mainland in the near future, it has already been recorded on the Channel Islands. It feeds on species of Brassicaceae, including cultivated and wild cabbages and less frequently grasses (Poaceae)

Eurydema herbaceum (Herrich-Schäffer, 1934)   This species is similar to *Eurydema oleracea* (page 76), but with broader areas of colour including a triangular patch in the centre of the corium. The larvae feed on Brassicaceae.

Pitedia juniperina (Linnaeus, 1758)   This species feeds on *Juniperus communis* and is very similar to *Piezodorus lituratus* (page 72), but it is bright green rather than yellow-green and has a much broader pale margin to the lateral edges of the pronotum.

Carpocoris purpureipennis (De Geer, 1773)   A large (11 to 14mm) reddish-brown bug with dark lateral points to the pronotum. A rare vagrant in the southern counties. The food plants include species of Apiaceae and mulleins *Verbascum* spp. There are other very similar species in Europe that may turn up in the southern counties of Britain. A modern European key would be necessary to identify any of the *Carpocoris* spp.

Species List

The following two pages list the native species of shieldbugs and squashbugs under their family headings. Former residents, migrants and some vagrants are also listed.

The list follows the scientific names used in the recent field key by Bernard Nau, *Guide to the Shieldbugs of the British Isles* (FSC Publication, Aidgap Guide. 2004)

Pentatomoidea

Acanthosomatidae
Acanthosoma haemorrhoidale (Linnaeus, 1758)
Cyphostethus tristriatus (Fabricius, 1787)
Elasmostethus interstinctus (Linnaeus, 1758)
Elasmucha grisea (Linnaeus, 1758)

No longer resident

   Elasmucha ferrugata (Fabricius, 1787)

Scutelleridae

Odontoscelis fuliginosa (Linnaeus, 1761)
Odontoscelis lineola Rambur, 1839
Eurygaster maura (Linnaeus, 1758)
Eurygaster testudinaria (Geoffroy, 1785)

No longer resident

   Eurygaster austriaca (Schrank, 1776)

Cydnidae

Legnotus limbosus (Geoffroy, 1785)
Legnotus picipes (Fallén, 1807)
Geotomus punctulatus (Costa, 1847)
Tritomegas bicolor (Linnaeus, 1758)
Canthophorus impressus Horvath, 1871
Sehirus biguttatus (Linnaeus, 1758)
Sehirus luctuosus Mulsant & Rey, 1866

Vagrant

   Cydnus aterrimus (Forster, 1771)

Thyreocoridae

Thyreocoris scarabaeoides (Linnaeus, 1758)

Pentatomidae

Podops inuncta (Fabricius, 1775)
Sciocoris cursitans (Fabricius, 1794)
Aelia acuminata (Linnaeus, 1758)
Neottiglossa pusilla (Gmelin, 1789)
Eysarcoris fabricii (Kirkaldy, 1904)
Eysarcoris aeneus (Scopoli, 1763)
Palomena prasina (Linnaeus, 1761)
Dolycoris baccarum (Linnaeus, 1758)
Piezodorus lituratus (Fabricius, 1794)
Pentatoma rufipes (Linnaeus, 1758)

Eurydema oleracea (Linnaeus, 1758)
Eurydema dominulus (Scopoli, 1763)
Picromerus bidens (Linnaeus, 1758)
Troilus luridus (Fabricius, 1775)
Rhacognathus punctatus (Linnaeus, 1758)
Zicrona caerulea (Linnaeus, 1758)

Recently naturalised

Nezara viridula (Linnaeus, 1758)

Migrants and vagrants

Dyroderes umbraculatus (Fabricius, 1775)
Jalla dumosa (Linnaeus, 1758)
Byrsinus flavicornis (Fabricius, 1794)
Carpocoris purpureipennis (De Geer, 1773)
Holcostethus vernalis (Wolff, 1804)
Eurydema herbaceum (Herrich-Schäffer, 1934)
Eurydema ornatum (Linnaeus, 1758)

No longer resident

Pitedia juniperina (Linnaeus, 1758)

Coreoidea

Coreidae

Gonocerus acuteangulatus (Goeze, 1778)
Coreus marginatus (Linnaeus, 1758)
Syromastes rhombeus (Linnaeus, 1767)
Enoplops scapha (Fabricius, 1794)
Spathocera dahlmanni (Schilling, 1829)
Bathysolen nubilus (Fallén, 1807)
Arenocoris falleni (Schilling, 1829)
Arenocoris waltli (Herrich-Schäffer, 1834)
Ceraleptus lividus Stein, 1858
Coriomerus denticulatus (Scopoli, 1763)

Life History Tables

The following tables detail the life history of each of the native shieldbugs and squashbugs. The columns are as follows:

the scientific name (abbreviated in two cases)

the life stage during the months between March and October

the most commonly recorded food plants

some typical habitats in which the species is found

The following symbols are used within the table:

a - adult

o - ova

l - larva

? - these stages are uncertain, as the lifecycle is incompletely known

The text is in bold when the adult is most abundant.

Species	Mar	Apr	May	Jun	Jul	Aug	Sept	Oct	Food type	Habitat
Acanthos. haemorrhoidale	a	a ao	ao ao	aol aol	aol	a la	la la	a la	Crataegus monogyna	Woods, hedges
Cyphostethus tristriatus	a	a a	a a	ao ao	ol ol	la la	la la	la a	Juniperus, Cupressus	Downs, gardens
Elasmosteth. interstinctus	a	a a	ao ao	aol aol	—	la la	a a	al a	Betula, Corylus	Woods, parks
Elasmucha grisea	a	a a	ao ao	aol ol	ol ol	la a	a a	a a	Betula species	Woods, parks
Odontoscelis fuliginosa	—	— —	— —	la la	ao ao	al —	— —	— —	Erodium species	Sandy areas
Odontoscelis lineola	—	— —	— —	la lao	ao aol	al —	— —	— —	Erodium species	Sandy areas
Eurygaster maura	a	a ao	ao aol	— —	— —	la a	a a	a a	Poaceae, cereals	Dry grassland
Eurygaster testudinaria	a	a ao	ao aol	al —	la —	a a	a a	a a	Juncus, Carex species	Damp grassland
Legnotus limbosus	a	a a	a ao	ao —	— —	— a	la a	a a	Galium species	Dry banks
Legnotus picipes	a	a ao	ao ao	aol aol	al la	a a	a a	a a	Galium species	Dry, sandy soil
Geotomus punctulatus	a	a ao	ao ol	ol la	a a	a a	a a	a a	Galium verum	Sand dunes
Tritomegas bicolor	a	a ao	ao aol	aol aol	ola la	la la	la a	a a	Lamium album	Hedges/woods
Canthophorus impressus	a	a a	ao aol	aol —	la a	a a	a a	a a	Thesium humifusum	Calcareous grassland
Sehirus biguttatus	a	a a?	a? ao?	ao? al?	I? I?	I? a	a a	a a	Melampyrum species	Woodland edge
Sehirus luctuosus	a	a a	a ao	ao al	I la	a a	a a	a a	Myosotis species	Downland
Thyreocoris scarabaeoides	a	a a	a ao	ao o	ol —	la la	a a	a a	Viola species	Short turf, sand
Podops inuncta	a	a a	a ao	ao ol	— —	la la	a a	a a	Poaceae	Grassland
Sciocoris cursitans	a	a ao	ao aol	aol —	— a	a a	a a	a a	Pilosella, Potentilla	Dry slopes, sand
Aelia acuminata	a	a a	ao aol	aol al	al la	la a	a a	a a	Poaceae	Grassland
Neottiglossa pusilla	a	a ao	ao ao	o —	— la	la a	a a	a a	Poa species, Poaceae	Damp grassland
Eysarcoris fabricii	a	a ao	ao aol	aol ol	ol la	la la	la la	la a	Stachys sylvatica	Woods, hedges
Eysarcoris aeneus	a	a ao	ao ao	aol aol	— —	la a	a a	a a	Hypericum pulchrum	Woods, heaths

Species	Mar	Apr	May	Jun	Jul	Aug	Sept	Oct	Food type	Habitat
Palomena prasina	a	a	ao	aol	aol	la	la	a	Trees, shrubs	Woods, gardens
Nezara viridula	a	a	ao?	?	?	—	a	a	Rosaceae, vegetables	Parks, gardens
Dolycoris baccarum	a	a	a	ao	al	la	la	a	*Prunus spinosa*	Scrub
Piezodorus lituratus	a	a	a	aol	—	la	la	a	*Ulex* species	Gorse scrub
Pentatoma rufipes	—	—	—	la	la	aol	al	al	*Quercus*, other trees	Woods, orchards
Eurydema oleracea	a	a	ao	la	a	a	al	al	Brassicaceae	Hedges, scrub
Eurydema dominulus	a	a	ao	ol	—	la	a	a	Brassicaceae	Woods, scrub
Picromerus bidens	o	o	o	ol	la	la	ao	ao	Lepidoptera, etc.	Woods, hedges
Troilus luridus	a	a	ao	ol	la	la	a	a	Lepidoptera, etc.	Woodland
Rhacognathus punctatus	a	a	ao	aol	—	la	a	a	*Lochmaea* species	Heathland
Zicrona caerulea	a	a	ao	ol	la	a	a	a	Chrysomelidae	Downland, heaths
Gonocerus acuteangulatus	a	a	a	ao	ol	la	a	a	*Buxus sempervirens*	Scrub, woodland
Coreus marginatus	a	a	ao	ao	la	la	a	a	*Rumex* species	Wasteland, herbs etc.
Syromastes rhombeus	a	a	ao	aol	—	—	a	a	*Spergularia* species	Sandy heaths
Enoplops scapha	a	a	aol	aol	la	la	a	a	Compositae species	Coastal dry vegetation
Spathocera dahlmanni	a	a	a	ao	la	la	a	a	*Rumex acetocella*	Dry sandy soil
Bathysolen nubilis	a	a	ao	ao	la	a	a	a	*Medicago lupulina*	Shingle, quarries etc.
Arenocoris falleni	a	a	ao	—	la	la	a	a	*Erodium* species	Coastal dunes
Arenocoris waltli	a	a	ao?	l?	l?	a	a	a	*Erodium* species	Sandy areas, dunes
Ceraleptus lividus	a	a	a	al	ol	la	a	a	*Trifolium* species	Sand dunes, commons
Coriomeris denticulatus	a	a	a	ol	—	la	a	a	*Trifolium* species	Quarries, gravel pits

References and Bibliography

Barclay, M.V.L., The Green Vegetable Bug *Nezara viridula* (Linnaeus, 1758) (Hemiptera: Pentatomidae) new to Britain. (Entomologist's Rec.J.Var. 116, 55-58., 2004)

Blamey, Marjorie., Fitter, Richard and Fitter, Alastair. Wild Flowers of Britain and Ireland (A & C Black Publishers Ltd. 2003)

British Red Data Books. No 2. Insects. (Nature Conservancy Council, 1987)

Brooke, Sheila E. The Southern Green Shield Bug, *Nezara viridula* (L.,1758) (Het News, Iss. 4, Autumn 2004, 2nd Series)

Butler, E.A. A Biology of the British Hemiptera – Heteroptera. (Witherby, 1923)

Chinery, Michael. Collins Pocket Guide. Insects of Britain and Western Europe (Harper Collins. 1986)

Chinery, Michael. Garden Wildlife of Britain and Europe (Collins Nature Guides. Harper Collins. 1997)

Dolling, W.R. The Hemiptera (OUP. 1991)

Douglas, J.W., and Scott, John. The British Hemiptera. Volume 1. Heteroptera (The Ray Society. 1865)

Gibbons, Bob. Collins Wild Guide to Insects of Britain and Europe (Harper Collins. 1999)

Hawkins, Roger D., Shieldbugs of Surrey (Surrey Wildlife Trust. 2003)

Jones, Hugh P., An Account of the Hemiptera - Heteroptera of Hampshire and the I. of Wight (The Entomologist's Rec.J.Var., 1934)

Kirby, Peter. A review of the scarce and threatened Hemiptera of Great Britain (JNCC. 1992)

Massee, A.M., The Hemiptera - Heteroptera of Kent, (Transactions of the Society for British Entomology Vol.11 part 12, 15th November 1954)

Nau, Bernard. Guide to the Shieldbugs of the British Isles (FSC Publication, Aidgap Guide. 2004)

Sauer, Frieder. Wanzen und Zikaden (Fauna Verlag, Goecke & Evers, 1996)

Shardlow, M.E.A. & Taylor, R. The Southern Green Shield Bug *Nezara viridula* (Linnaeus,1758) (Hemiptera: Pentatomidae) – another species colonising Britain due to climate change? (*British Journal of Entomology & Natural History.* 2004)

Southwood, T.R.E., and Leston, Denis. Land and Water Bugs of the British Isles (Frederick Warne & Co: Wayside and Woodland Series. 1959)

Villiers, Andre. Hemipteres de France (Societe Nouvelle des Editions Boubee & Co. 1977)

Zahradnik, Jiri., Severa, Frantisek. and Polak, Jiri. A Field Guide in Colour to Insects (Blitz. 1998)

Index

The following pages index the shieldbugs, squashbugs, plants and prey types in this guide. The numbers in bold indicate the page number of the detailed species account.